Little Mitchie

HOW DO FISH BREATHE UNDERWATER?

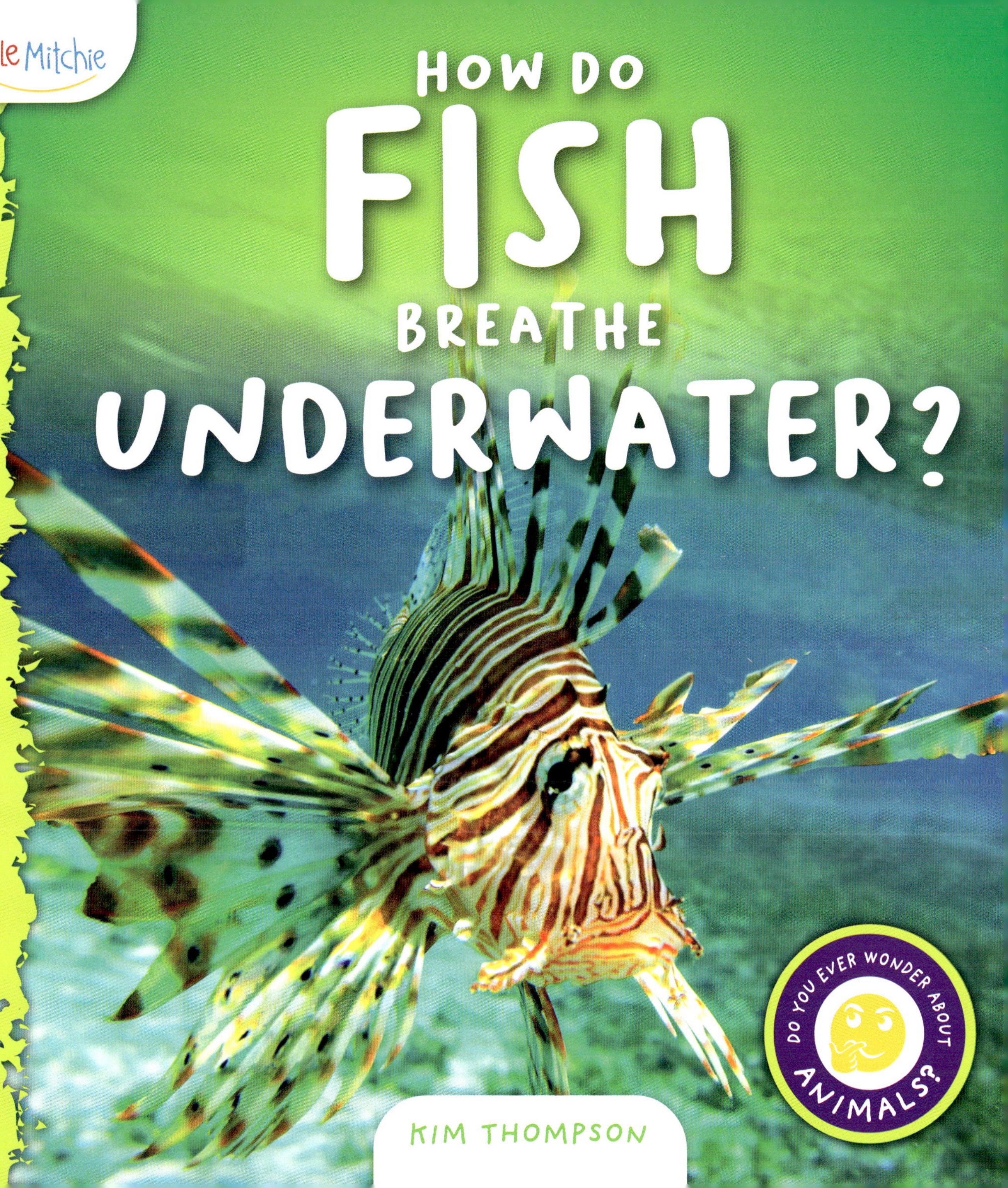

DO YOU EVER WONDER ABOUT ANIMALS?

KIM THOMPSON

CREATING YOUNG NONFICTION READERS

Little Mitchie books spark curiosity and support early nonfiction reading for students in Grades 2-3. Designed to build vocabulary, support second language learners, and prepare readers for middle-grade content, each book includes helpful tips for parents and educators to build confidence and deepen understanding of the world.

TIPS FOR READING NONFICTION WITH BEGINNING READERS

Talk about Nonfiction

Begin by explaining that nonfiction books give us information that is true. The book will be organized around a specific topic or idea, and we may learn new facts through reading.

Look at the Parts

Most nonfiction books have helpful features. Our *Little Mitchie* titles include color photographs and graphic aids, a table of contents, a glossary, and an index. Share the purpose of these features with your reader.

Color Photos and Graphic Aids

A lot of information can be found by "reading" photos, charts, maps, and other graphic aids found within nonfiction texts. Help your reader learn more about the different ways information can be displayed.

Table of Contents

Located at the front of the book, this list shows the big ideas within the text and the page numbers where they can be found.

Glossary

Located at the back of the book, the glossary defines key words and phrases that are related to the topic. These words and phrases can be found in the text in colored type.

Index

Located at the back of the book, an index is an alphabetical list of topics and the page numbers where they can be found.

With a little help and guidance about reading nonfiction, you can feel good about introducing a young reader to the world of *Little Mitchie* nonfiction books.

Little Mitchie is an imprint of:

Mitchell Lane
PUBLISHERS

2001 SW 31st Avenue
Hallandale, FL 33009
mitchelllanepub.com

First Edition, 2027.

Author: Kim Thompson
Designer: Jen Bowers

Library of Congress Cataloging-in-Publication Data
Title: How Do Fish Breathe? / by Kim Thompson

Description: Hallandale, FL :
Mitchell Lane Publishers, [2027]

Identifiers:
ISBN 979-8-89260-923-4 (library bound)
ISBN 979-8-89260-978-4 (eBook)

Library of Congress Control Number: 2026936352

PHOTO CREDITS
Shutterstock: cover, p.1 ©2014 Pakhnyushchy, p.5 ©2020 Katelyn Redlin, p.6–7 ©2016 Mirek Kijewski, p.9 ©2018 Ken Kiefer, p.10–11 ©2018 koliw, p.13 ©2019 Noheaphotos, p.14 ©2007 ivvv1975, p.17 ©2019 Elizaveta Obukhova, p.18–19 ©2019 Rich Carey, p.21 ©2016 Rich Carey, p.22 ©BlueRingMedia

TABLE OF CONTENTS

Chapter One

QUESTIONS

Have you ever looked closely at a fish? Did you notice a flap on either side of its head?

You probably wondered about those flaps. You may have asked these questions.

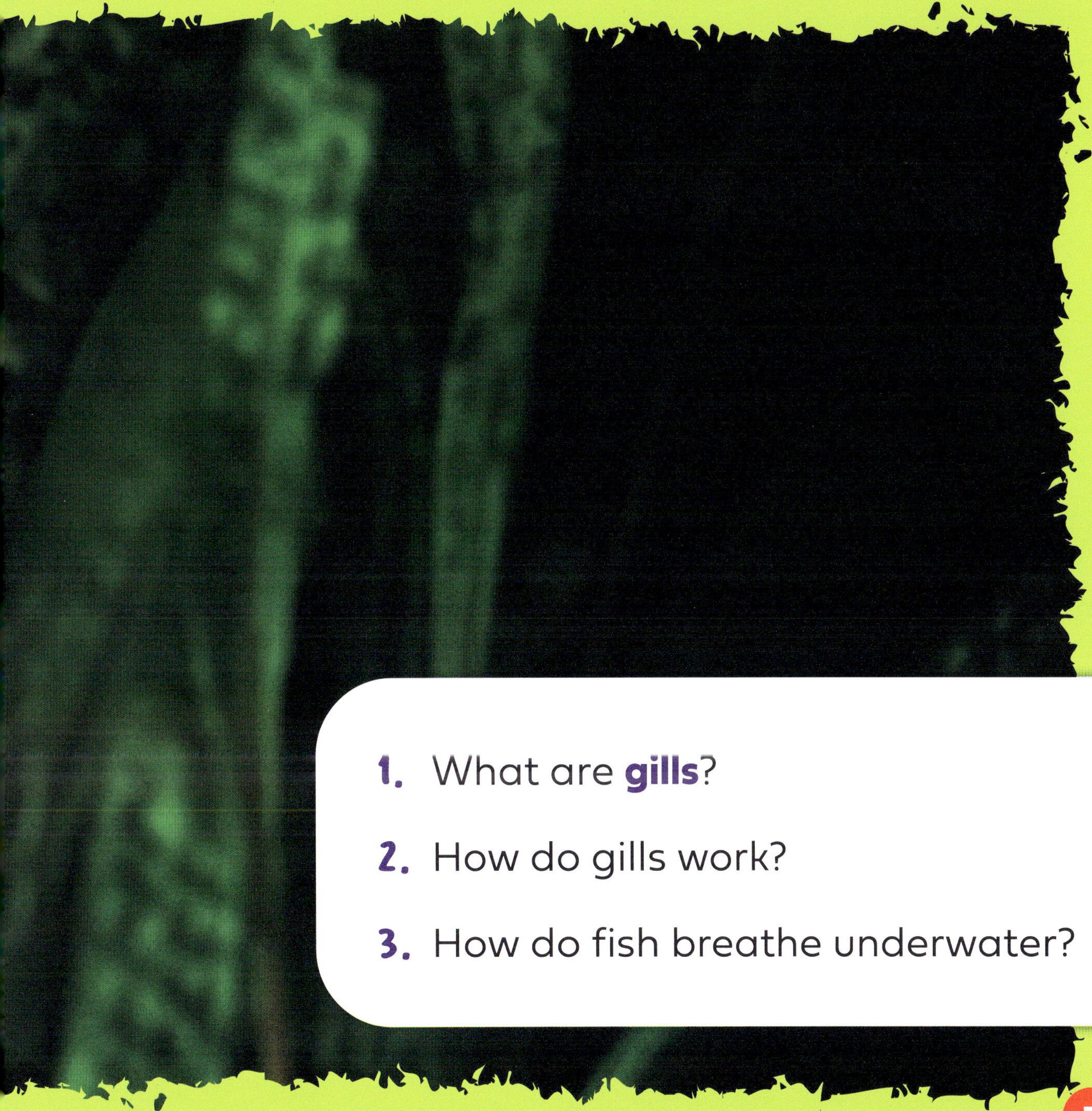

1. What are **gills**?
2. How do gills work?
3. How do fish breathe underwater?

Chapter Two

UNDER THE FLAPS

A fish's bony flaps are gill covers. They protect the gills underneath. These **organs** are very **delicate**. Most fish have two pairs of gills behind each flap.

ANIMAL WONDER

A shark is a fish, but it doesn't have gill covers. It has at least five open gill slits on each side of its body.

Each gill is shaped like an arch. Thin **filaments** branch out from the arch. They are covered with tiny blood vessels called **capillaries**.

Chapter Three

TAKING AND GIVING

A fish closes its gill flaps. Water flows into its open mouth.

The fish opens its gill flaps. The water gets sucked out through the flaps. First, though, it passes over the gills.

ANIMAL WONDER

Animals can't live without **oxygen**. It helps them break down food. It helps them move and grow.

The gills take oxygen from the water. It goes into the bloodstream. It flows through the fish's body.

The gills give off **carbon dioxide**. It is **waste**. It goes into the water escaping through the gill flaps.

Chapter Four

BREATHING WATER

Lungs help people **absorb** oxygen from air. Gills help fish absorb oxygen from water. In other words, people breathe air. Fish breathe—you guessed it—water!

ANIMAL WONDER

Gills can absorb three-quarters of the oxygen in a "breath" of water. Lungs absorb oxygen from a breath of air at a much lower rate.

Deep water has less oxygen. Fish that swim there must take in more water to get the oxygen they need. They can pull water over their gills 80 times in a minute.

ANIMAL WONDER

Polluted water also contains less oxygen. Keeping water clean helps fish breathe.

Chapter Five

ANSWERS

Now, you can answer your questions.

1. **WHAT ARE GILLS?**

   Gills are fish organs covered in tiny blood vessels.

2. **HOW DO GILLS WORK?**

   As water flows over them, gills take oxygen from the water and give off waste.

3. **HOW DO FISH BREATHE UNDERWATER?**

   Fish breathe water that contains the oxygen they need to live.

ANIMAL WONDER

Keep asking questions about animals. That's how you learn about the amazing creatures that share our world!

FISH GILL DIAGRAM

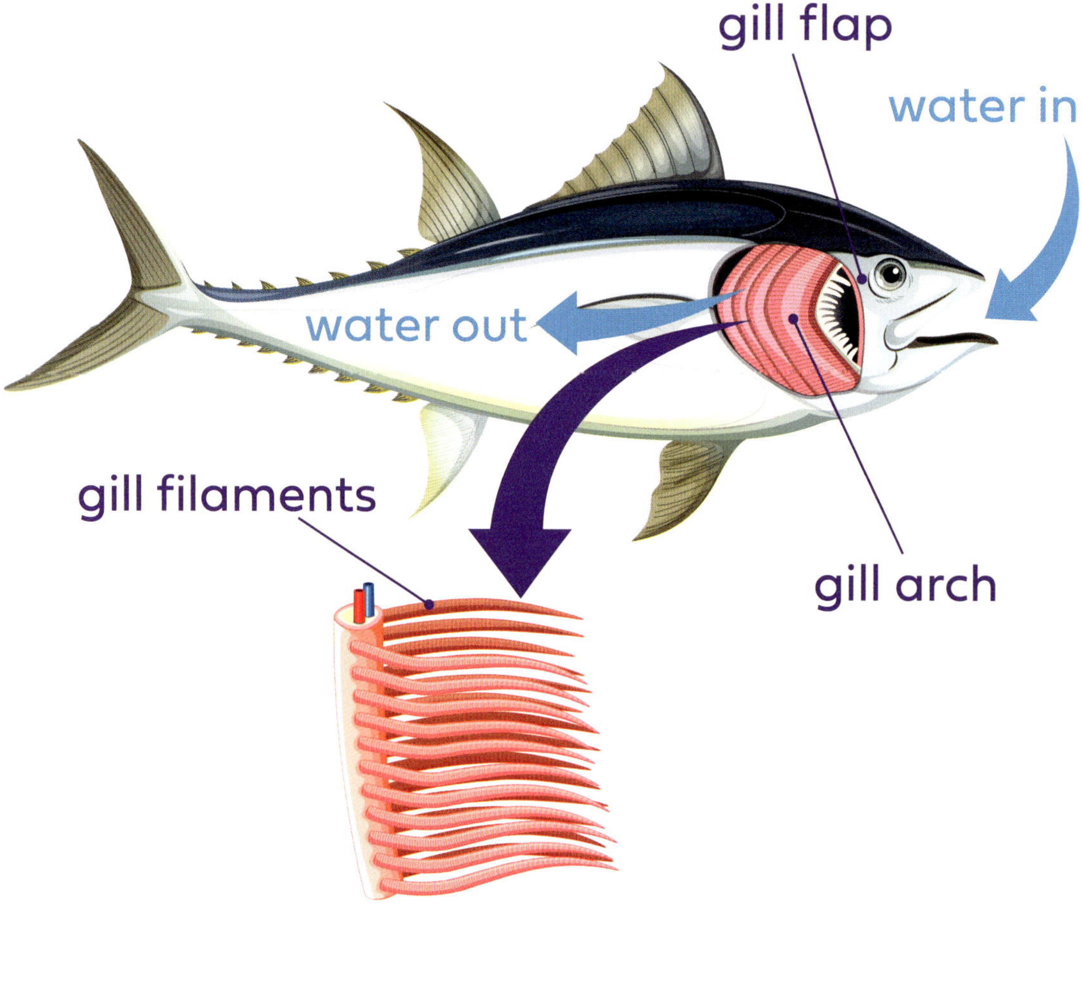

GLOSSARY

absorb (ab-ZORB) to soak up or take in

capillaries (KAP-uh-ler-eez) small tubes that transfer blood between arteries and veins

carbon dioxide (KAHR-buhn dye-AHK-side) a gas made up of carbon and oxygen that people and animals breathe out and that plants take in

delicate (DEL-i-kit) finely made or sensitive; fragile

filaments (FIL-uh-muhnts) very fine threads

gills (gilz) organs near the mouth that fish use to breathe underwater

lungs (luhngz) baglike organs inside the chest that allow people and animals to breathe air

organs (OR-guhns) parts of the body, such as the heart or liver, that have specific purposes

oxygen (AHK-si-juhn) a gas that has no color, that is found in air and water, and that people and animals need to breathe in to stay alive

waste (wayst) something that is left over and not needed

FURTHER READING

Hume, Sam. *An Anthology of Aquatic Life.* DK Children, 2022.

Lindholm, Jane. *Do Fish Breathe Underwater and Other Silly Questions from Curious Kids.* Grosset and Dunlap, 2022.

ON THE INTERNET

Fun Kids Live: Top 10 Facts about Fish!
funkidslive.com/learn/top-10-facts/top-10-facts-about-fish
Learn fascinating fish facts.

SciShow Kids: How Do Fish Breathe?
youtube.com/watch?v=zj5v3n6Nlm8
Learn more about how fish breathe underwater.

Smithsonian Marine Station: What's a Fish?
youtube.com/watch?v=Ozz3X-P3HhQ
Learn what makes fish different from all other animals.

INDEX